A New True Book

FOSSILS

By Allan Roberts

This "true book" was prepared
under the direction of
Illa Podendorf,
formerly with the Laboratory School,
University of Chicago

CHILDRENS PRESS, CHICAGO

Plant fossil (Annularia stellata)

PHOTO CREDITS

Root Resources: ©Louise K. Broman—cover, 2, 8 (2 photos), 10 (2 photos), 34 (2 photos), 43 (right)

Allan Roberts—6 (2 photos), 13 (2 photos), 15, 16, 19 (2 photos), 21 (2 photos), 27 (left), 28, 30, 33 (2 photos), 36, 38 (2 photos), 42, 44 (top and bottom right)

Lynn M. Stone—4 (top), 40, 44 (bottom right)

Joseph A. DiChello, Jr.—41

James P. Rowan—29

Kitty Kohout—43 (bottom left)

Connecticut Department of Economic Development—4 (bottom)

Reinhard Brucker—18 (2 photos), 24, 43 (top left)

Field Museum of Natural History—23, 32

Smithsonian Institution: National Museum of Natural History—27 (right)

COVER—Forty-million-year-old fossil fish found in Green River, Wyoming

Library of Congress Cataloging in Publication Data

Roberts, Allan.
  Fossils.

  (A New true book)
  Includes index.
  Summary: Explains how the remains of an animal or plant fossilize over millions of years, where fossils may be found, and what we can learn from them.
  1. Paleontology—Juvenile literature.
[1. Paleontology. 2. Fossils] I. Title.
QE714.5.R58 1983   560   82-23521
ISBN 0-516-01678-4   AACR2

Copyright © 1983 by Regensteiner Publishing Enterprises, Inc.
All rights reserved. Published simultaneously in Canada.
Printed in the United States of America.
1 2 3 4 5 6 7 8 9 10 R 92 91 90 89 88 87 86 85 84 83

TABLE OF CONTENTS

What Is a Fossil?... 5

What Happens to Dead Animals and Plants?... 7

How Are Fossils Formed?... 11

Petrified Fossils... 14

Fossils in Amber... 20

Fossils in Ice... 23

Fossils in Tar... 26

Fossils of Carbon... 28

Other Interesting Fossils... 30

Collecting Fossils... 35

Fossils Are Important... 39

Words You Should Know... 46

Index... 47

Two fossils: tree bark (left), leaf (right)

Dinosaur footprints in Connecticut

WHAT IS A FOSSIL?

A fossil is the remains of an animal or plant. A fossil can be thousands or millions of years old!

Fossils can be bones. They can also be tracks, tunnels, or other "signs" left by ancient life.

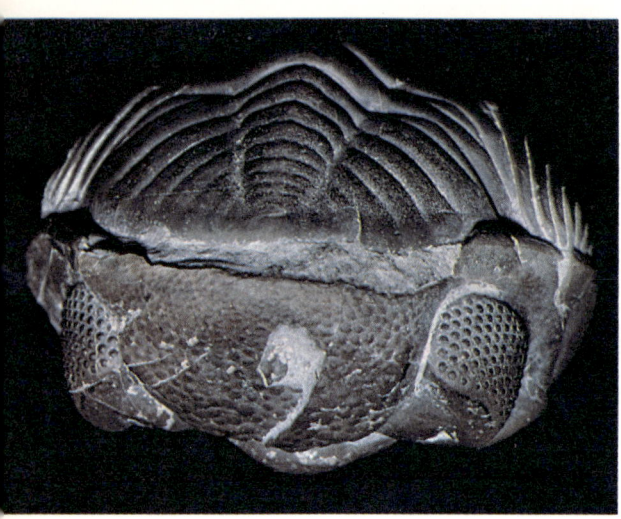

Above: Front view of trilobite (TRY • low • byte) showing compound eyes. Right: Close-up of the skull of a flesh-eating dinosaur, Gorgosaurus (gor • guh • SORE • us), that lived 75 million years ago.

Fossils tell us what life was like on earth long ago.

The study of fossils is called paleontology.

WHAT HAPPENS TO DEAD ANIMALS AND PLANTS?

All animals and plants die.

After dying, animals and plants are first eaten by "scavengers." Vultures, turtles, crabs, and insects eat dead animals. They are scavengers. Insects eating dead wood are also scavengers.

These scavengers often will eat the complete animal or plant.

Even if scavengers do not eat the dead animal or plant, it will usually still disappear completely because of "decay."

Decay is caused by bacteria. The bacteria break down the plant or animal tissues into chemicals. These chemicals then return to the soil or water.

Above: Insect fossil
Left: Seed fern fossil

No fossils can be formed if all the remains are eaten by scavengers or destroyed by bacteria.

Millipede (MIL • ih • peed) fossil

Crab fossil found in sandstone

HOW ARE FOSSILS FORMED?

Fossils can be formed in many ways. Sometimes mud or sand covers the dead animal or plant. When the "soft" parts of the animal or plant decay, the mud or sand will fill in the empty "spaces."

Hard parts, such as shells, bone, or wood, will sometimes not decay. They will stay in the mud. Over a long period of time, the mud might turn into rock.

Shale is a rock that used to be mud. Sandstone is a rock that used to be sand. Many fossils have been found in both these types of rock.

Left: Sandstone is a sedimentary rock.
Above: Slate is a metamorphic rock formed from sediments such as shale or clay.

Rocks made from mud or sand are called sedimentary rocks. Most fossils are found in sedimentary rocks.

PETRIFIED FOSSILS

Some fossils, or remains, are turned into stone. This happens when bone or wood is covered with wet mud and sand. In time, water slowly dissolves the chemicals in the bone or wood cells.

These old chemicals are slowly replaced with other chemicals. Over a long period of time the bone or wood is completely

Petrified wood has been changed to stone.

changed into stone.
Petrified fossils of dinosaur bones and wood have been found.

Dinosaur bones uncovered in the Morrison formation in Dinosaur National Monument

In Dinosaur National Monument you can watch scientists digging up petrified fossils.

This place once was a bend in an ancient river. As the animals died, their bones were covered with wet sand. In time their bones were petrified.

Above: Dimetrodon (DY • metra • don) skeleton
Right: Skeleton of Tyranosaurus Rex (ty • ran • ah • SORE • us REX)

    Many of these bones have been put together. Today complete dinosaur skeletons can be seen in many museums!

    Bones of small horses, hogs, camels, and even rhinos have been found at

Above: Turtle shell fossil from Badlands National Park
Left: Petrified wood from the Petrified Forest National Park

Badlands National Park in South Dakota. Even entire petrified turtle shells have been uncovered.

If you wish to see beautiful fossil trees, visit Petrified Forest National Park in Arizona.

FOSSILS IN AMBER

Amber is hardened resin. Resin is the "juice" inside evergreen trees. Today we use the resin of pine trees to make turpentine.

Whenever trees are injured, resin oozes out. Resin is sticky. Many insects, spiders, and millipedes are trapped by this resin.

Left: Resin oozing out of modern pine tree
Above: Ant trapped in amber millions of years ago

Millions of years ago animals were trapped in resin. They did not decay. In time the resin became hard and turned into amber.

Some of these fossils have been found in amber. Each hair, eye, and leg of the insect has been perfectly preserved.

This process of making fossils is still taking place today. Just think, the insects caught in resin today might become some of the fossils of the future.

FOSSILS IN ICE

The bodies of woolly mammoths have been uncovered in the icy frozen ground of Alaska and Siberia.

Ice Age in Europe showing woolly mammoths and rhinoceroses

The Eskimos used to feed the meat of these frozen fossils to their dogs. At one time nearly half of the world's supply of ivory came from the tusks of fossil mammoths.

Skeleton of woolly mammoth

The frozen blood vessels, muscles, hair, skin, stomachs, and other body organs of these mammoths have been preserved and studied.

Some of these mammoths are in museums. In order to keep them frozen, they are put in large freezers with glass fronts.

FOSSILS IN TAR

Fossils have been found in tar pits.

In some places, natural tar oozes up out of the ground and even forms pools of tar.

Since water can also be found in these places, the animals once probably came here to drink.

Some were trapped in the sticky tar. Many died there. The bones of ground

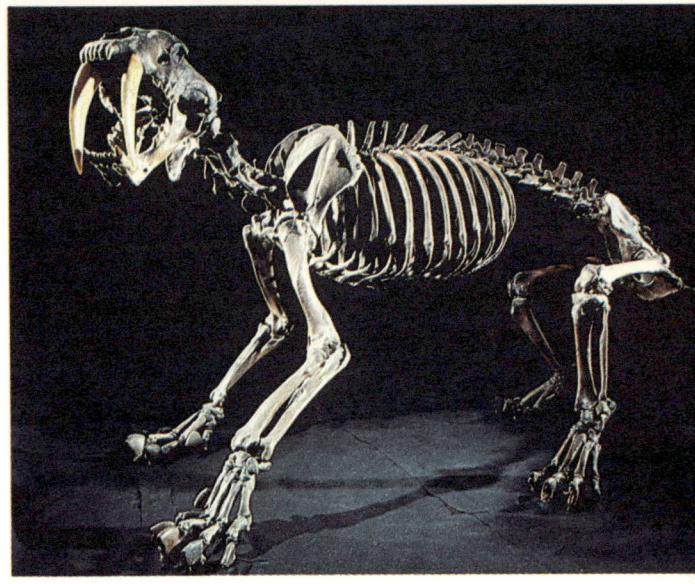

Fossils of extinct elephants and saber-toothed cats have been found at LaBrea Tar Pits in California. Models have been put in tar pits to show visitors how these prehistoric creatures were trapped in tar.

sloths, mammoths, saber-toothed tigers, bears, antelope, camels, geese, and eagles have been found in tar pits. Large insects fossilized in tar have also been discovered.

Fossilized sweetgum leaf

FOSSILS OF CARBON

All living animals and plants have carbon in their bodies. When some plants and fish were turned into fossils, this carbon was left in the rocks. A perfect

Fossil fish

imprint of a leaf or fish in rock might also be "black" in color. This black color is what is left of the carbon that the animal or plant had inside of it while living long ago.

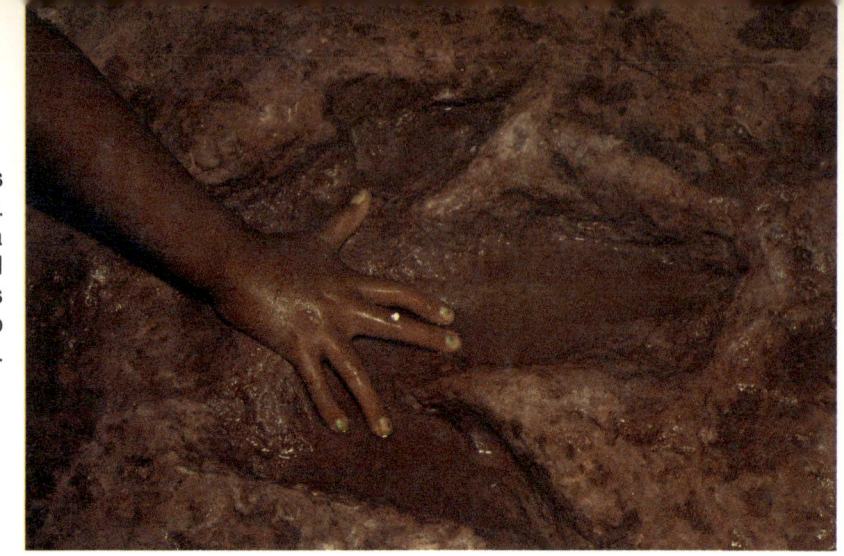

Dinosaur tracks in sandstone. The hand of a three-year-old Indian girl is shown to demonstrate size.

OTHER INTERESTING FOSSILS

If a crab, bird, or dinosaur walked across soft mud or sand, it sometimes left its footprints. A few of these footprints are now preserved in stone. This is because the mud or sand was later turned into rock.

Thousands of insects live in dead wood today. Other insects did the same thing millions of years ago.

Thousands of pieces of petrified wood have been found that show the tunnels made by ancient insects. Of course, these tunnels were made before the wood was petrified.

Protoceratops was a dinosaur about five to six feet long. It used to lay eggs in the sand, as turtles do today.

Some of these eggs were found fossilized from 75 million years ago.

Protoceratops (pro • toh • SAIR • ah • tops) display at the Field Museum of Natural History in Chicago

Close-up of the skull of a Protoceratops (left) and its fossilized eggs (above)

Scientists have opened some of these "rock eggs." To their surprise they discovered some of the eggs contained the petrified bones of unborn baby dinosaurs.

Using geological hammers scientists uncovered the annularia (ann • uh • LAIR • ee • ya) plant fossil shown below.

COLLECTING FOSSILS

Many governments have laws to stop people from digging up rare fossils, such as dinosaurs. They let only scientists dig for them because they know how to correctly remove the bones.

However, there are millions of common fossils in the earth. Many of them you can collect.

Above: Buttermilk Falls in New York State
Right: Snake River in Grand Teton National Park

The best place to look for fossils are where different "layers" of rock can be seen.

Look where roads cut through hills and mountains. Look along stream beds.

Always take an adult along with you. Also, ask permission from the owner of the land before looking for fossils. Many times the owner, or other local people, will show you the best places to look.

Be careful. Rock ledges might break, causing you to fall.

You can also find fossils at "fossil and rock shows." It is here that people gather to sell and trade their fossil "finds."

Tree ferns (above) are living fossils. Fossils of tree ferns have been found dating from the Coal Age in prehistoric times (below).

FOSSILS ARE IMPORTANT

Fossils are important. Have you ever heard anyone talk about "fossil fuel?" Gas, coal, and oil are fossil fuels. They have been made by fossil deposits of plants and animals!

We need fossil fuels. We heat our buildings and homes with them. They are used to run our buses, cars, trains, ships, and airplanes, too.

We use fossils to show us where to drill for the oil and gas we need.

Many buildings are made of stone. Limestone is a

Shells in limestone

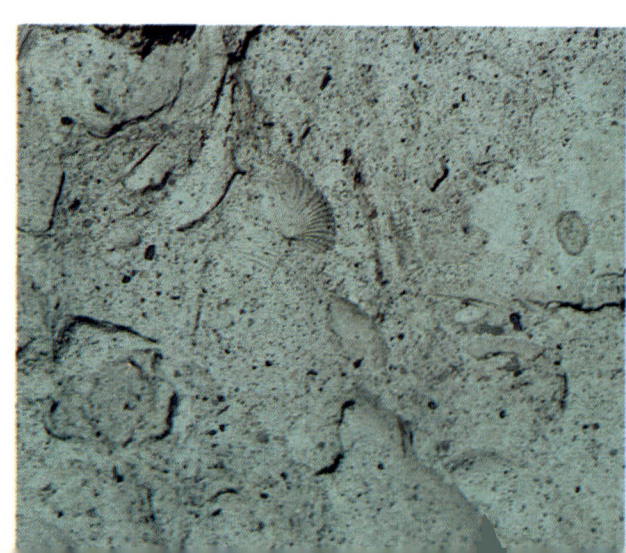

The Rare-book Library at Yale University has marble panels.
Marble is made from limestone.

Sea life as it was about 400 million years ago.

rock formed by the remains of ancient animals and plants of the oceans.
 Even the chalk that you use at school is made from the remains of tiny fossils.

Some of the prettiest scenery in the world is the result of rocks formed by dead animals and plants.

Above right: Fossil shells
Top left: Petrified wood
Left: Plant fossil

Above: Model of a fossil dragonfly that lived during the Coal Age. The wings of this prehistoric dragonfly were two-and-a-half feet across. Right: Model of archaeopteryx (are • kay • OP • ter • ix), the first bird. Below: Student examines a fossil.

Every fossil can tell us a story of past life as it used to be. Without fossil deposits, we would know very little about the plants and animals that lived millions of years ago. Our knowledge of the history of the earth would be incomplete.

WORDS YOU SHOULD KNOW

ancient (AIN • shent) — of times long ago
carbon (KAR • bun) — a chemical element found in all living things
decay (dee • KAY) — to rot
embryo (EM • bree • oh) — a plant or animal when it is just beginning to develop from a seed or egg
extinct (ex • TINKT) — no longer existing; died out
gully (GULL • ee) — a ditch cut in the earth by flowing water
fossil (FAWSS • ill) — the remains or traces of a plant or animal that lived long ago
imprint (IM • print) — a mark, pattern, or design made by pressing something on a surface
metamorphic (meh • ta • MOR • fik) **rock** — rock that has been changed physically by heat, pressure, and water into a finer more compact form
paleontology (pail • ee • en • TAHL • oh • gee) — the study of fossils
petrified (PET • rih • fyed) — changed into stone
preserve (prih • ZERVE) — to save; to keep
rare (RAIR) — not found or seen very often; unusual
resin (REH • zin) — a sticky substance that comes from certain trees or other plants
scavenger (SCAV • en • jer) — an organism that feeds on dead matter
sedimentary (sed • ih • MEN • ter • ee) **rock** — a type of rock made from small pieces of matter that were once in water
silica (SILL • ih • kah) — a chemical found in some types of rocks
tissue (TIH • shoo) — a group of plant or animal cells that are alike

INDEX

age of fossils, 5
Alaska, 23
amber, fossils in, 20-22
animals, after dying, 7-9, 11, 17, 21, 26, 28, 29, 39, 43
antelope, 27
Arizona, 19
bacteria, cause of decay, 8, 9
Badlands National Park, 19
bears, 27
bird fossils, 27, 30
bones, 12, 14, 15, 17, 18, 26, 33
camel fossils, 18, 27
carbon, fossils of, 28, 29
chalk, 42
coal, 39
collecting fossils, 35-37
crabs, 7, 30
dead animals, 7-9, 11, 17, 21, 26, 28, 29, 39, 43
dead plants, 7-9, 11, 28, 29, 39, 43
decay, of plants and animals, 8, 11
definition of fossil, 5
Dinosaur National Park, 17
dinosaurs, 15, 17, 18, 30, 32, 33, 35
eagles, 27
eggs, fossilized, 32, 33

Eskimos, 24
finding fossils, 36, 37
fish fossils, 28
footprints, fossils of, 30
formation of fossils, 11-13
fossil fuels, 39, 40
fuels, fossil, 39, 40
gas, 39, 40
geese, 27
ground sloths, 18
horse fossils, 18
ice, fossils in, 23-25
insects, 7, 20, 22, 27, 31
ivory, from tusks of fossils, 24
leaf fossils, 29
limestone, 40
mammoths, woolly, 23-25, 27
millipedes, 20
mud, 11-14
museums, 18, 25
oil, 39, 40
paleontology, 6
Petrified Forest National Park, 19
petrified fossils, 14-19, 31
plants, after dying, 7-9, 11, 28, 29, 39, 43
protoceratops, 32
resin, fossils in, 20, 21
rhinoceros fossils, 18, 23
rock, formed from mud, 12, 13

rock, formed from sand, **12, 13**
"rock eggs," **32, 33**
saber-toothed tigers, **27**
sand, **11-14, 17**
sandstone, **12**
scavengers, **7-9**
sedimentary rocks, **13**
shale, **12**
shells, **12**
shows, fossil and rock, **37**
Siberia, **23**
South Dakota, **19**

spiders, **20**
stone, fossils turned into, **14, 15**
tar, fossils in, **26, 27**
tar pits, **26, 27**
tigers, saber-toothed, **27**
tree, fossils, **19**
tree resin, **20**
turtle fossils, **19**
turtles, **7, 32**
vultures, **7**
wood, **12, 14, 15, 31**
woolly mammoths, **23-25, 27**

About the Author

Allan Roberts received his undergraduate degree from Earlham College. As a participant in the National Science Foundation Academic Year Institute, he received his master's degree from the University of Georgia. Currently a biology teacher at Richmond High School in Richmond, Indiana, Allan has taught for more than twenty-three years. In addition to his regular classroom activities, he has taught at Indiana Extension University and special classes for the young. Many of his research articles and photographs have been published. His photographs also have appeared in the National Geographic, Reader's Digest, Audubon, National Wildlife *and many textbooks.*

A New True Book

COWBOYS

By Teri Martini

This "true book" was prepared
under the direction of
Illa Podendorf,
formerly with the Laboratory School,
University of Chicago

CHILDRENS PRESS, CHICAGO

PHOTO CREDITS

© 1981 James Fain, Logan, Utah—cover, 2, 7, 13, 17, 19 (bottom), 23, 24 (4 photos), 28, 29, 32, 34, 41, 44 (top), 45

Texas State Department of Highways and Public Transportation—4, 8, 10 (2 photos), 12, 14, 15, 19 (2 photos at top), 21, 35, 38, 42, 44 (bottom)

Bobbie Lieberman, Equus Magazine—26 (above)

John McDonald, Equus Magazine—26 (below)

Randy Huffman, Crockett, Texas—30, 33 (2 photos), 40

United States Department of Agriculture—37

Cover—Cattle Drive, Utah

Library of Congress Cataloging in Publication Data

Martini, Teri.
  Cowboys.

  (A New true book)
  Rev. ed. of: The true book of Cowboys.
  SUMMARY: Briefly describes the clothing cowboys wear; their duties on the ranch, range, and roundup; and their recreation at rodeos.
  1. Cowboys—Juvenile literature. 2. West (U.S.)—Social life and customs—Juvenile literature. 3. Ranch life—West (U.S.)—Juvenile literature. [1. Cowboys] I. Title.
F596.M33   1981   978   81-10049
ISBN 0-516-01611-3   AACR2

Copyright © 1981 by Regensteiner Publishing Enterprises, Inc.
All rights reserved. Published simultaneously in Canada.
Printed in the United States of America.
Original Copyright © 1955, Childrens Press
      3 4 5 6 7 8 9 10 R 90 89 88 87 86 85 84 83

TABLE OF CONTENTS

Cowboys and Their Horses... **5**

Spring Round-up... **9**

Branding the Calves... **20**

Summer on the Ranch... **25**

Rodeos... **29**

Fall Round-up... **34**

Winter on the Range... **36**

Cowboy Clothes... **39**

Words You Should Know... **46**

Index... **47**

COWBOYS AND THEIR HORSES

Cowboys take care of cattle. The cowboys work on ranches.

Often the cattle ranch has miles and miles of open land. This is the range. The cattle wander far to find grass.

For hundreds of years the cowboys and their horses have looked after cattle.

Today there are not many cowboys. And machines do some of a cowboy's work. But cowboys and their horses still are needed.

SPRING ROUND-UP

Today the cowboys get up early. It is time for the spring round-up.

Each cowboy has a horse. He keeps the horse in a corral or barn.

But there are other horses on the ranch. They wander with the cattle.

The cowboys saddle up their horses. They ride out to find the other horses. They bring them back to the corral.

Cowboys eat well before round-up.

The next morning the cowboys start the round-up.

The cowboys take along the extra horses. The horses are needed for the round-up.

Saddling up the horses

Taking a break on the range

During the round-up the cowboys live outside. They ride all day to the place where they will camp. They get their supper. Then they go to sleep under the stars.

One of the cowboys is always awake. He is called the nighthawk.

The next morning the cowboys ride "circle." This means they ride off in a wide circle to look for the cattle.

A cowboy finds some cows with calves. He rides around them. He waves his hat. This is called hazing. This is the way he drives them into camp.

Sometimes cowboys use aircraft to find the cattle.

The cowboys know their cattle by the mark or brand on the side. The brand shows who owns the cattle. It takes a few days to find them. When all the cattle are in camp, the calves are branded. They also are given medicine. This helps keep them well.

BRANDING THE CALVES

A cowboy rides in between the calf and its mother. This is called cutting out the calves. A lasso drops over the calf's head. The horse stands still and holds the rope tight.

The cowboy jumps down. He ties three of the calf's legs together. Another cowboy touches the calf's side with a hot iron. The calf is branded.

Then the calf jumps up. It runs off to find its mother.

At last all the calves are branded. The cattle are turned loose again. So are the extra horses. Then the cowboys ride for home.

Cowboys going home

A cowboy and his dog look after the cattle. The horses get looked after, too. The cowboy at lower right looks at his horse's hoofs. The cowboy below is shaping a new horseshoe.

SUMMER ON THE RANCH

In summer there is much work for the cowboys. Some go on the range to watch the cattle. Some mend fences. Others train horses.

The young horses are called yearlings. In summer they are brought in off the range. Cowboys work with the yearlings. Soon they become used to people. When they are older they will learn to carry a rider.

Bull riding

RODEOS

Cowboys do not work all of the time. One of the things they do for fun is go to the rodeo. The best cowboys enter contests.

Calf roping

There is calf roping. The winner ropes a calf and ties its legs in the shortest time.

There is bulldogging. The cowboy throws a steer off its feet by twisting its horns.

Some of the cowboys ride bucking broncos. Some ride Brahma bulls.

Rodeos once were just a fun time for cowboys. Now some cowboys don't work on ranches anymore. They go to rodeos to win money and prizes.

FALL ROUND-UP

Fall comes. It is round-up time again.

This time full-grown cattle are rounded up. They are driven to a feed lot. They are put on trucks by the people who buy them.

The cattle are healthy.
They bring a good price.
The cowboys have done
their work well.

WINTER ON THE RANGE

In winter, the cowboys look after the cattle still on the range. They give the cattle salt. When it snows the cattle can't eat grass. So the cowboys take the cattle hay to eat.

COWBOY CLOTHES

A cowboy's clothes are good clothes for the work he does. His big hat shades his eyes. It helps keep his head cool. And he can use it to wave at cattle who are trying to run away.

Boots help cowboys keep their feet in the stirrups.

A stirrup

Cowboy boots have small tips and high heels. The tips let the boots fit into a stirrup easily. The heels keep the boots from slipping. The boots' leather sides protect a cowboy from snake bites.

Sometimes he also wears leather pants legs. These are chaps. They protect his legs from sharp bushes.

He needs a warm shirt. He is outside a lot.

Cowboys work hard all year round. They take care of cattle. They take care of the ranch. And their rodeos are for fun.

WORDS YOU SHOULD KNOW

Brahma (BRAH•muh) — a kind of bull

brand — a mark burned into an animal's skin to show who owns it

bucking bronco (BUHK•ing BRONK•oh) — a horse that jumps upward and forward

bull-dogging — to throw an animal to the ground by grabbing the horns and twisting the head

calf (KAF) — a young cow or bull

chaps — heavy leather pants without a seat that are put over regular pants to protect the legs

corral (kuh•RALL) — an area with a fence around it where animals are kept

cutting out — to ride a horse between a calf and its mother so as to separate them

haze (HAYZ) — to drive cattle back into their camp by making loud noises and waving things at them

lasso (LASS•oh) — a long rope with a loop at one end used to catch animals

nighthawk — the cowboy who stays awake and watches at night

range (RAYNJ) — a large, open area of land where animals feed on the plants

rodeo (ROH•dee•oh) — a show where cowboys enter contests like cattle roping, bronco riding, and other events

round-up — to gather animals together

yearling (YEER•ling) — an animal in its second year

INDEX

aircraft, 18
barn, 9
boots, cowboy, 41
Brahma bulls, 32
branding, 18, 20, 22
bucking broncos, 32
bull-dogging, 31
calf roping, 31
calves, 17, 18, 20, 22
calves, branding, 18, 20, 22
calves, cutting out, 20
camp, 15, 17, 18
cattle, 5, 6, 11, 16-18, 20, 22, 25, 34, 35, 36, 39, 45
cattle ranches, 5, 11, 45
chaps, 43
"circle" riding, 16
clothes, cowboy, 39-43
corral, 9, 11
cowboy clothes, 39-43
cows, 17
cutting out the calves, 20
fall round-up, 34, 35
feed lot, 34
fences, mending, 25

grass, 5, 36
hat, cowboy, 17, 39
hay, 36
hazing, 17
horses, 6, 9, 11, 12, 20, 22, 25, 27
lasso, 20
medicine, for calves, 18
nighthawk, 16
ranches, 5, 11, 45
range, 5, 25, 27, 36
riding "circle," 16
rodeos, 29-32, 45
roping calves, 31
round-up, fall, 34, 35
round-up, spring, 9-18
salt, 36
snakes, 41
spring round-up, 9-18
steer bull-dogging, 31
stirrups, 41
summer work, 25, 27
winter work, 36
yearling horses, 27

About the Author

Teri Martini is a teacher turned writer. Her titles in the True Book series grew out of specific needs she saw in her elementary school classrooms. She has a Masters Degree in education from Columbia University. Among the 22 books she has written, 14 are for children. Her short stories and articles have appeared in Scott Foresman Basic Readers, Childcraft, Scholastic Publications, and 'Teen Magazine. At present she divides her time between writing and teaching other writers to write for children through The Institute of Children's Literature in Redding Ridge, Connecticut. She is listed in Who's Who of American Women, Contemporary Authors and The International Dictionary of Biography.